Surrender

A Devotional

Steve Harris

Surrender
A Devotional

Third Impression – December 2023
First Published in English in 2008 and Mandarin in 2010.

Published by Global Influencers
PO Box 308, Morningside QLD 4170, Australia
www.globalinfluencers.org

Copyright © 2008, 2021 by Steve Harris and Outpouring Ministries
All rights reserved

ISBN 978-0-6450343-7-0 (paperback)
ISBN 978-0-6450343-4-9 (eBook)

This book or parts thereof may not be reproduced in any form, stored in a retrieval system, or transmitted in any form by any means - electronic, mechanical, photocopy, recording, or otherwise - without prior written permission of the publisher, except as provided by Australian copyright law.

1 **In Your Will**

2 **Sanctuary (Living Sacrifice)** (available on CD "Overflow"
https://steveharris.hearnow.com/overflow

3 **Wherever You Lead**
1,2,3 Words & Music Copyright © 1996, 1998, 2008 Steve Harris

Bible Versions Used

Unless otherwise indicated, Scripture quotations are taken from the **New American Standard Bible®** **(NASB)**, Copyright © 1960, 1962, 1963, 1968, 1971, 1972, 1973, 1975, 1977, 1995 by The Lockman Foundation. Used by permission.
www.Lockman.org

Scripture quotations marked **(NIV)** are taken from the **Holy Bible, New International Version®, NIV®**. Copyright © 1973, 1978, 1984, 2011 by Biblica, Inc.™ Used by permission of Zondervan. All rights reserved worldwide.
www.zondervan.com The "NIV" and "New International Version" are trademarks registered in the United States Patent and Trademark Office by Biblica, Inc.™

Surrender

The LORD is our Strength
and our Song (**Exodus 15:2**).

Our future belongs to Him
(**Jeremiah 29:11, Isaiah 49:15-16,
1 Corinthians 6:19-20**),
not to anyone else;
because it truly is our God
Who through various ways
and means, faithfully provides
all of our needs through
His limitless provision that
is found in His Glory
(**Philippians 4:19-20**).

In the sight of men, we may be nothing
(and remember Jesus willingly
made Himself nothing - **Philippians 2:3-7**).

But, in the sight of God, we are
His precious children (**1 John 3:1-2**).

He has awesome and amazing things
planned for those who love Him
and who are called and living
according to His glorious purpose
(**Romans 8:28-31**).

But we must be willing to be obedient
and submitted to the **fullness** of His will
- which **always** involves death
(**Isaiah 6:5-8, Luke 9:23,
1 Corinthians 15:31, Philippians 2:8-11**).

Yet, for those who are willing to fall
to the ground and die, GOD **can** and **will** bring
forth an abundant increase from
that DEAD SEED
(**John 12:24-25**).

Yes, this is the wonder and mystery
and mastery of our God.

He constantly and consistently
(there is no shadow of turning in Him - **James 1:17**)
brings forth abundant and eternal life
from death (**John 3:16, John 5:24-25**).

He brings forth beauty
from ashes
and the oil of joy
from mourning;

He creates the garment of praise where
previously there was a spirit of heaviness

so that

we can be witnesses of and
to His Splendor and Glory
to the ends of the earth
(**Isaiah 61:1-3**).

All glory, honor, worship, and praise
to our mighty everlasting God

Who sits forever on the Throne
of Heavenly Radiant Glory (**Revelation 4:1-5**).

LORD, may the whole earth
be filled with Your Glory
just as the waters cover the sea
(**Numbers 14:21, Habakkuk 2:14**)!

And may we, Your servants,
having passed through
the Valley of the
Shadow of Death (**Psalm 23:4**)

and

the Valley of Tears
(**Psalm 84:6-7**),

bring pleasure
to Your beautiful heart
as we willingly lay down
our lives for You in love
and devoted service
(**Psalm 116:12-15**).

Selah

and

Amen.

~oOo~

As we learn to continually
and consistently abide in Him,
so He will joyfully
and continually abide with us.
(Isaiah 57:15, 66:1-2)

And there is simply no greater joy
this side of Heaven than to be
in the centre of the will of God,
serving Him all the days of our lives,
and all for His glory.

I pray that you will know great
joy, peace and fulfillment
as you learn to truly
and unconditionally
surrender your all to Him.

~oOo~

The only way to truly know the fullness
of His Glory is through the laid-down life of a lover;
one who is so surrendered to Him that joy
is found even in the sharing of His sufferings.
(Philippians 2:17, 3:7-14)

In Your Will [1]

Not by might, nor by power
Not my will, but Yours be done
Lead me by still waters
By Your Holy Spirit, O God

In Your will there is joy
and everlasting peace
There is hope and fullness of life
In Your will, LORD we share
in Your perfect love
LORD, I want to do Your will

LORD, I want to be Your servant
Following You all of my days
So fill my heart to overflowing
LORD, lead me in all of Your ways

In Your will there is joy
and everlasting peace
There is hope and fullness of life
In Your will, LORD we share
in Your perfect love
LORD, I want to do Your will

Wherever You Lead [2]

LORD I worship You
And I seek Your face
In the beauty of
the Most Holy Place

As I walk in the light
Of Your infinite Grace
By Your Spirit I know
I will finish the race

For Your Word
to Your servant
Has given me hope
Your command
has set my heart free

I have counted the cost
I will take up the cross
I will be who
You've called me to be

LORD, I'll follow
wherever You lead

Living Sacrifice [3]

Behold a door
Standing open in Heaven
We see the King of Glory there
LORD, I'm on my way
And when I meet You there

I will worship You
In Spirit and Truth
In the sanctuary
Of Your holiness

At the cross
My Saviour is waiting
His grace and mercy
Draw me there
LORD, You paid the price
You gave Your life

So I present myself
A living sacrifice
And I will praise and
glorify You with my life

Jesus, my Savior
You're my Oil of Joy
My King
You are my everything

I will worship You
In Spirit and Truth
In the sanctuary
Of Your holiness

I present myself
A living sacrifice
And I will praise and
Glorify You with my life

Surrender Has a Cost

I'll never forget one very special evening that I was woken up by the audible voice of the LORD. He was speaking His word to me, from **Philippians 3:14**, in a loud, audible, and booming voice :

"forgetting those things which are behind, and pressing towards the goal for the prize of the upwards call of God in Christ Jesus."

These words were repeated audibly to me, by Jesus, over and over; they saturated the atmosphere of the house, until the morning sun began to lighten the sky.

I'll never forget the moment that I first encountered those verses – it was years before the Divine encounter. At the time, I'd only been a Christian for nine months or so.

I'll also never forget the awe that I felt for God and also for the obedience of His servant Paul and his willingness to press inward and onward and upward into God and into his Divine call - regardless of the cost.

Paul was often misunderstood, mocked, and beaten, just like His Saviour, and it was often by those who felt that they were God's "appointed guardians of the truth…"

I also knew – as such a young believer - that what I was reading was a reflection in part of what my own journey with Christ would look like, although as a baby Christian I had no idea of what "the sufferings of Christ" would actually entail.

I remember getting down on my knees and saying "LORD, I want to know You as Your servant Paul did. I want to know the power of Your resurrection, and even the fellowship of Your sufferings..."

- because, even as a 'baby' Christian, I somehow knew that the suffering that would come through obedience to Christ was also the way that would lead to supernatural, glorious, abundant life and open Heavenly doors - not just for me, but for thousands and tens of thousands and even hundreds of thousands all over the world.

Oh, how much 'easier' it could be to be a 'believer' rather than a 'disciple' ... but, Called Out and Chosen One, you know what He is calling you to do !

Jesus says that if we truly love Him, we will do so much more than just receive from Him, in fact that we will take up our crosses and follow Him (**Mark 8:34**). Jesus also said that we show our love for Him, and our friendship with Him, by obeying His commands (**John 15:12-14**), and His primary command is simply to "go".

As I read **Philippians 3:7-14** on that special morning, I wept ...for many reasons. Our walk as disciples of Jesus Christ **will** be costly, and in fact, the Bible guarantees that the walk of a disciple of Christ will have accompanying persecutions (**2 Timothy 3:12**).

But - the cost that we are called upon to pay (and it will be different for each of us) is just so worth it, to simply show our love for Him – and then, through Christ in us (**Galatians 2:20; Colossians 1:27**), to be able to snatch those who are perishing out of the fire and to help them to set their own feet upon the Solid Rock of Christ.

This is solid food, not milk ... where oh where is our treasure ? Who – and what - is it that truly makes our heart beat faster, and captures our undying focus, our resources, and our time ?

There is always a deeper level of surrender that God is calling us to. It is always costly, and sometimes very painful, but always glorious.

No matter how rocky the road may seem at times, remain steadfast in your call – forgetting those things which are behind, and reaching forward to those things which are ahead.

Continue to press toward the goal for the prize of the upward call of God in Christ Jesus.

You will not be disappointed.

~oOo~

There was another occasion when I was leading a group of pastors into a place of deep worship. I was sitting at the grand piano and singing spontaneous songs that were coming from the realms of Glory.

Suddenly, God released a visible and weighty Glory into the room. I looked up briefly at one point and saw that every person in the room had been slain in the Spirit. Some were sobbing very quietly into the carpet.

As I turned back to the piano, something extraordinary happened. A very large timber cross had suddenly appeared with its foundations set into the music stand. The accompanying Glory was so intense that I fell forward on to the cross, weeping.

Somehow I managed to stretch my arms forward to embrace the cross, and as I did, I could actually feel the rough timber and large, rough splinters. The Divine love accompanying this encounter was completely overwhelming. The pain of the splinters was intensely real.

Out of the middle of the Glory, a booming Heavenly voice filled with overwhelming love spoke to me and said, "Steve, the only way into the Glory is through a willingness to share in my sufferings."

Let us surrender absolutely everything to Him, and resolve meet Him in the Glory, regardless of the cost.

Surrender – a Devotional
Scripture References

Psalm 73:24 (NIV)
You guide me with your counsel,
and afterward You will take me into glory.

Philippians 3:7-14
[7] But whatever things were gain to me, these things I have counted as loss because of Christ.

[8] More than that, I count all things to be loss in view of the surpassing value of knowing Christ Jesus my LORD, for whom I have suffered the loss of all things, and count them mere rubbish, so that I may gain Christ, [9] and may be found in Him, not having a righteousness of my own derived from the Law, but that which is through faith in Christ, the righteousness which comes from God on the basis of faith, [10] that I may know Him and the power of His resurrection and the fellowship of His sufferings, being conformed to His death; [11] if somehow I may attain to the resurrection from the dead.

¹² Not that I have already grasped it all or have already become perfect, but I press on if I may also take hold of that for which I was even taken hold of by Christ Jesus.

¹³ Brothers and sisters, I do not regard myself as having taken hold of it yet; but one thing I do: forgetting what lies behind and reaching forward to what lies ahead, ¹⁴ I press on toward the goal for the prize of the upward call of God in Christ Jesus.

Exodus 15:2
The LORD is my strength and song,
And He has become my salvation;
This is my God, and I will praise Him;
My father's God, and I will exalt Him.

Jeremiah 29:11-13
¹¹ "For I know the plans that I have for you,"
declares the LORD, "plans for prosperity
and not for disaster, to give you
a future and a hope.

¹² Then you will call upon Me and come
and pray to Me, and I will listen to you.

[13] And you will seek Me and find Me
when you search for Me with all your heart."

Isaiah 49:15-16
[15] "Can a woman forget her nursing child
And have no compassion on the son of her womb?
Even these may forget, but I will not forget you.
[16] Behold, I have inscribed you on the palms of
My hands; Your walls are continually before Me."

Philippians 2:3-7
[3] Do nothing from selfishness or empty conceit,
but with humility consider one another as more
important than yourselves; [4] do not merely look
out for your own personal interests, but also
for the interests of others.

[5] Have this attitude in yourselves which was also
in Christ Jesus, [6] who, as He already existed in
the form of God, did not consider equality with
God something to be grasped, [7] but emptied
Himself by taking the form of a bond-servant
and being born in the likeness of men.

1 Corinthians 6:19-20

[19] Or do you not know that your body is a temple of the Holy Spirit within you, whom you have from God, and that you are not your own?
[20] For you have been bought for a price: therefore glorify God in your body.

1 John 3:1-2

[1] See how great a love the Father has given us, that we would be called children of God; and in fact we are. For this reason the world does not know us: because it did not know Him.

[2] Beloved, now we are children of God, and it has not appeared as yet what we will be. We know that when He appears, we will be like Him, because we will see Him just as He is.

Luke 9:23

And He was saying to them all,
"If anyone wants to come after Me,
he must deny himself, take up his cross daily,
and follow Me."

Romans 8:28-31

²⁸ And we know that God causes all things to work together for good to those who love God, to those who are called according to His purpose.

²⁹ For those whom He foreknew, He also predestined to become conformed to the image of His Son, so that He would be the firstborn among many brothers and sisters; ³⁰ and these whom He predestined, He also called; and these whom He called, He also justified; and these whom He justified, He also glorified.

³¹ What then shall we say to these things? If God is for us, who is against us?

1 Corinthians 15:31

I affirm, brothers and sisters, by the boasting in you which I have in Christ Jesus our LORD, that I die daily.

Isaiah 6:5-8

⁵ Then I said, "Woe to me, for I am ruined!
Because I am a man of unclean lips,
And I live among a people of unclean lips;
For my eyes have seen the King,
the LORD of armies."

⁶ Then one of the seraphim flew to me
with a burning coal in his hand, which he had taken
from the altar with tongs.

⁷ He touched my mouth with it and said,
"Behold, this has touched your lips; and your guilt
is taken away and atonement is made for your sin."

James 1:17

Every good gift and every perfect gift
is from above, and cometh down
from the Father of lights,
with Whom is no variableness,
neither shadow of turning. **(KJV)**

John 3:16

"For God so loved the world, that He gave
His only Son, so that everyone who believes
in Him will not perish, but have eternal life."

Philippians 2:8-11
⁸ And being found in appearance as a man,
He humbled Himself by becoming obedient
to the point of death : death on a cross.

⁹ For this reason also God highly exalted Him,
and bestowed on Him the name which is above
every name, ¹⁰ so that at the name of Jesus every
knee will bow, of those who are in heaven and
on earth and under the earth, ¹¹ and that every
tongue will confess that Jesus Christ is LORD,
to the glory of God the Father.

John 12:24-25
²⁴ Truly, truly I say to you, unless a grain
of wheat falls into the earth and dies,
it remains alone; but if it dies, it bears much fruit.
²⁵ The one who loves his life loses it,
and the one who hates his life in this world
will keep it to eternal life.

Isaiah 61:1-3 (NIV)
The Spirit of the Sovereign LORD
is on Me, because the LORD
has anointed Me to preach good news to the poor.

He has sent me to bind up the brokenhearted,
to proclaim freedom for the captives and release
from darkness for the prisoners, to proclaim
the Year of the LORD's Favor and the Day
of Vengeance of our God, to comfort all who mourn,
and provide for those who grieve in Zion - to bestow
on them a crown of beauty instead of ashes, the oil
of gladness instead of mourning, and a garment of
praise instead of a spirit of despair.

They will be called oaks of righteousness, a planting
of the LORD for the display of His splendor.

Revelation 4:1-5

¹After these things I looked, and behold,
a door standing open in heaven,
and the first voice which I had heard,
like the sound of a trumpet speaking with me, said,
"Come up here, and I will show you
what must take place after these things."

² Immediately I was in the Spirit; and behold, a throne was standing in heaven, and someone was sitting on the throne. ³ And He who was sitting was like a jasper stone and a sardius in appearance; and there was a rainbow around the throne, like an emerald in appearance.

⁴ Around the throne were twenty-four thrones; and upon the thrones I saw twenty-four elders sitting, clothed in white garments, and golden crowns on their heads.

The Throne and Worship of the Creator

⁵ Out from the throne *came flashes of lightning and sounds and peals of thunder. And there were seven lamps of fire burning before the throne, which are the seven spirits of God.

Numbers 14:21
"…however, as I live, all the earth
will be filled with the glory of the LORD."

Habakkuk 2:14
For the earth will be filled with the knowledge
of the glory of the LORD, as the waters cover the
sea.

Psalm 23:4
Even though I walk through
the valley of the shadow of death,
I fear no evil, for You are with me;
Your rod and Your staff,
they comfort me.

Psalm 84:6-7
⁶ Passing through the Valley of Baca
they make it a spring; the early rain
also covers it with blessings.

⁷ They go from strength to strength,
Every one of them appears before God in Zion.

Psalm 116:12-15

¹² What shall I repay to the LORD
For all His benefits to me?
¹³ I will lift up the cup of salvation,
And call upon the name of the LORD.

¹⁴ I will pay my vows to the LORD;
May it be in the presence of all His people!
¹⁵ Precious in the sight of the LORD
Is the death of His godly ones.

Isaiah 57:15

For this is what the high and exalted One
Who lives forever, whose name is Holy, says:

"I dwell in a high and holy place,
And also with the contrite and lowly of spirit
In order to revive the spirit of the lowly
And to revive the heart of the contrite."

Isaiah 66:1-2

This is what the LORD says:
"Heaven is My throne and the earth
is the footstool for My feet.

Where then is a house you could build for Me?
And where is a place that I may rest?

²For My hand made all these things, so all these
things came into being," declares the LORD.

"But I will look to this one,
at one who is humble and contrite in spirit,
and who trembles at My word.

Philippians 2:17

¹⁷But even if I am being poured out
as a drink offering upon the sacrifice
and service of your faith,
I rejoice and share my joy with you all.

INVITATION TO MAKE YOUR PEACE WITH GOD

Dear Friend, it's possible that you have read this booklet because someone who loves you very much has given it to you. It's also possible that you have read this far, without knowing Jesus Christ as LORD, or without understanding that you need to make your peace with God.

If that is you, please read on, because I would like to explain to you how easy it is, and how wonderful it is, to receive Jesus Christ into your heart and into your life.

He wants to give you the free gift of eternal life, and it is as easy as sincerely believing in Him and sincerely receiving Him.

Step 1 - Understand that God has a plan for your life – and it's a good plan

His plan for you involves the free gift of true love, peace, joy, and abundant and eternal life.

Jeremiah 29:11 (NIV)
"For I know the plans I have for you," declares the LORD, "plans to prosper you and not to harm you, plans to give you hope and a future".

Romans 5:1 (NIV)
*We have peace with God
through our LORD Jesus Christ.*

John 3:16 (NIV)
*For God so loved the world
that He gave His only begotten Son,
that whoever believes in Him
should not perish but have everlasting life.*

John 10:10 (NIV)
*I (Jesus) have come that they may have life,
and that they may have it more abundantly.*

Step 2 - Understand that your life choices have separated you from God

God created us in His own image, and He gave each of us the gift of free will and free choice.

Unfortunately, most of us did not understand or appreciate this gift, and the choices that we have made have taken us far from the path of divine destiny and eternal love that was meant just for us.

This has resulted in separation from God and from His wonderful plan for our life.

The Bible says in **Romans 3:23** :-
For all have sinned and fall short of the glory of God.

And in **Romans 6:23 (NIV)** we read :-
*For the wages of sin is death, but the gift of God
is eternal life in Christ Jesus our LORD.*

Proverbs 14:12 (NIV) says :-
*"There is a way that seems right to a man,
but in the end it leads to death."*

Isaiah 59:2 (NIV)
*But your iniquities have separated you from your God;
your sins have hidden his face from you,
so that he will not hear.*

Step 3 - Understand that God has made a Way back to Himself through the Cross of Calvary

God knew that many, in ignorance of the truth, would walk away from Him. And so, He provided a way for us to return to Him. He sent His one and only beloved Son, Jesus Christ to die on the Cross as a sacrifice for our sins and wrong doing.

Because of His sacrifice, we can have peace with God, if we are willing to repent (change our way of thinking about God, ourselves, and others) and to receive His free gift of salvation.

Not only did Jesus die in our place and pay the penalty for our sins, but He defeated the power of death and rose from the grave.

He now personally invites each of us to follow Him into eternal life and eternal glory.

Romans 5:8 (NIV)
But God demonstrates his own love for us in this:
While we were still sinners, Christ died for us.

Colossians 1:19-22 (NIV)
For God was pleased ... through Him (Jesus)
to reconcile to Himself all things, whether things on earth
or things in heaven, by making peace through his blood,
shed on the cross.

Once you were alienated from God and were enemies
in your minds because of your evil behavior.

But now he has reconciled you by Christ's physical body
through death to present you holy in his sight,
without blemish and free from accusation.

1 Timothy 2:5 (NIV)
For there is one God and one mediator
between God and men, the man Jesus Christ.

Step 4 - Trust and believe God, and make your own decision to receive Christ into your heart, TODAY.

If you have read this far, it is because God is speaking directly to you, and He is calling you to take your rightful place as a member of His eternal family.

This is the most important decision of your life, and it is a decision that will activate God's gift of eternal life within you as soon as you make it. The best time to make this decision is – today.

Hebrews 4:7 (NIV)
Today, if you hear his voice, do not harden your hearts.

Romans 10:9 (NIV)
*If you confess with your mouth, 'Jesus is LORD,'
and believe in your heart that God raised Him
from the dead, you will be saved.*

John 1:12 (NIV)
*Yet to all who received him,
to those who believed in his name,
He gave the right to become children of God.*

Step 5 – Pray – Talk to God – Tell Him that you have decided to come back to Him

Prayer is talking to God. Your first prayer is your first conversation with your Creator, and through it, if your heart is sincere, He is about to give you the gift of eternal life. All you have to do is ask Him for it. Prayer simply means "talking with God." You can speak to Him through prayer in the same way that you speak to a person.

Please pray the following prayer, with a sincere heart. There is no need to feel shy or hesitant. Your Creator God has been waiting and longing for you to have this exact conversation with Him, since the beginning of time.

"LORD Jesus, I know that I am a sinner and that I need Your forgiveness. Today I choose to repent - to change my way of thinking about You, myself, and others.

I believe that You died for my sins. I want to turn from my sins and live a life that is pleasing to you. I want to live according to Your plan for my life, and I need Your help to do that.

I now invite You to come into my heart and life. I want to trust and follow You as LORD and Savior. I ask and pray this in Jesus' Name. Amen."

If you prayed this prayer sincerely, the Bible assures you (in **Romans 10:13 (NIV)**) that:-

Everyone who calls on the
Name of the LORD will be saved.

And in **Ephesians 2:8-9 (NIV)**
we have this assurance :-

For it is by grace you have been saved,
through faith - and this not from yourselves,
it is the gift of God - not by works,
so that no one can boast.

Congratulations, and welcome to the family of God! Your life will never be the same again.

The Bible says that angels are rejoicing right now because of your decision.

Luke 15:10
"In the same way, I tell you, there is rejoicing in the presence of the angels of God over one sinner who repents."

Now, it's essential that you continue to walk in the pathway of your new life as a member of the family of God. The next page contains some helpful advice to help you to do that.

How to Walk With God

Here are some important steps that will help you to grow and become a strong Christian :-

1) Obtain a Bible and read it every day;

2) Seek out the friendship and fellowship of other Christians who are walking strongly with God;

3) Talk to God in prayer every day;

4) Tell others about your decision to follow Jesus;

5) Ask the person who gave you this booklet, or other Christians that you may know, if they can help you to find a good local church where you can spend time with committed Christians, who can help you to grow stronger in your faith.

6) Find out about water baptism
(God will seal you as His own);

7) Find out about the Baptism of the Holy Spirit *(God will fill you with His divine power to live a powerful, supernatural life).* God bless you !

About the Author

Apostle Steve Harris has walked with Jesus since 1987. He has been blessed to worship with ministers such as Ron Kenoly and Pastor Benny Hinn. He has taught the Word of God and preached the Gospel of the Kingdom in many nations of the world, with salvation, healing, and miracles often accompanying the message.

As the founder of Outpouring Ministries (an organisation that exists to make a difference in a world full of desperate need), Steve has established mercy ministries in developing nations, constructing wells, computer and sewing schools, and establishing small to medium enterprises to permanently lift communities out of poverty.

He is also the founder of Global Influencers, a global community joined together in agape love and growing through the truth of God's Word and the fire of the Holy Spirit. Members are trained and equipped to walk in the fullness of the Gospel of the Kingdom, and to restore Kingdom culture from grassroots to government in the villages, cities, regions, and nations of the world.

Steve is commissioned through the Full Gospel Churches of Australia and ARC Global / H.I.M. He is the author of numerous books, and the composer of 3 worship CDs.

Worship CDs

www.globalinfluencers.org/resources
https://steveharris.hearnow.com
www.youtube.com/@steveharrisworship

Books

www.globalinfluencers.org/books

www.ingramcontent.com/pod-product-compliance
Lightning Source LLC
Chambersburg PA
CBHW032019290426
44109CB00013B/719